Praise for the Believe Series

"As grandparents of fifty grandchildren, we heartily endorse the *Believe and You're There* series. Parents and grandparents, gather your children around you and discover the scriptures again as they come alive in the *Believe and You're There* series."

—STEPHEN AND SANDRA COVEY
Stephen Covey is the bestselling author of *7 Habits of Highly Effective People*

"Bravo! This series is a treasure! You pray that your children will fall in love with and get lost in the scriptures just as they are discovering the wonder of reading. This series does it. Two thumbs way, way up!"

—MACK AND REBECCA WILBERG
Mack Wilberg is the Music Director of the Mormon Tabernacle Choir

"This series is a powerful tool for helping children learn to liken the scriptures to themselves. Helping children experience the scriptural stories from their point of view is genius."

—ED AND PATRICIA PINEGAR
Ed Pinegar is the bestselling author of *Raising the Bar*

"We only wish these wonderful books had been available when we were raising our own children. How we look forward to sharing them with all our grandchildren!"

—STEPHEN AND JANET ROBINSON

or of *Believing*

"The *Believe and You're There* series taps into the popular genre of fantasy and imagination in a wonderful way. Today's children will be drawn into the reality of events described in the scriptures. Ever true to the scriptural accounts, the authors have crafted delightful stories that will surely awaken children's vivid imaginations while teaching truths that will often sound familiar."

—TRUMAN AND ANN MADSEN
Truman Madsen was the bestselling author of *Joseph Smith, the Prophet*

"My dad and I read *At the Miracles of Jesus* together. First I'd read a chapter, and then he would. Now we're reading the next book. He says he feels the Spirit when we read. So do I."
—CASEY J., AGE 9

"My mom likes me to read before bed. I used to hate it, but the *Believe* books make reading fun and exciting. And they make you feel good inside, too."
—KADEN T., AGE 10

"Reading the *Believe* series with my tweens and my teens has been a big spiritual boost in our home—even for me! It always leaves me peaceful and more certain about what I believe."
—GLADYS A., AGE 43

"I love how Katie, Matthew, and Peter are connected to each other and to their grandma. These stories link children to their families, their ancestors, and on to the Savior. I heartily recommend them for any child, parent, or grandparent."
—ANNE S., AGE 50
Mother of ten, grandmother of nine (and counting)

When the White Dove Descended

When the White Dove Descended

Book 1

ALICE W· JOHNSON & ALLISON H· WARNER

DESERET
BOOK

Salt Lake City, Utah

Library of Congress Cataloging-in-Publication Data

Johnson, Alice W.

  Believe and you're there when the white dove descended / Alice W. Johnson, Allison H. Warner ; illustrated by Jerry Harston.

      p.   cm.

  ISBN-13: 978-1-59038-721-4 (pbk. : alk. paper)

  ISBN-10: 1-59038-721-X (pbk. : alk. paper)

  1. Jesus Christ—Baptism—Juvenile literature.   2. John, the Baptist, Saint—Juvenile literature.   I. Warner, Allison H.   II. Harston, Jerry ill. III. Title.

  BT350.J64 2007

  232.9'5—dc22

                                                                                    2007005792

Printed in the United States of America

Worzalla Publishing Co., Stevens Point, WI

10   9   8   7   6   5

Believe in the wonder,
Believe if you dare,
Believe in your heart,
Just believe . . . and you're there!

Contents

Chapter One

For Children Only

"No parents allowed," read the sign taped to Grandma's front door. "Say good-bye right here," Grandma instructed her grown-up daughter in a firm voice, but her eyes sparkled with merriment and fun. "You can pick up your children tomorrow night, and I'll have dinner ready for all of us," she promised.

Her three grandchildren dutifully waved good-bye to their mother. Then Katie, who at age twelve felt much older than her little brothers, took charge. "Matthew, Peter, pick up your suitcases and we'll all go in." With that, she

turned smartly and headed for the house, her blonde ponytail bobbing up and down with each step.

Almost-eight-year-old Peter, with his mop of wild brown curls flying (as usual) in all directions, bounded energetically behind her—without his suitcase. Matthew, age ten, smiled to

himself, picked it up along with his own, and joined the others.

"Grandma, did you know I'm a Cub Scout now?" Peter asked, taking Grandma's hand.

"Well, what do you know? I hadn't heard that," Grandma tousled his hair affectionately.

"Yup! I'm a Cub Scout! It's all I've ever lived

for!" he half-hollered with his trademark enthusiasm.

Grandma couldn't help thinking: *By the end of this weekend, Peter dear, I hope you will discover some even more important things to live for.*

Every year, for each of their birthdays, Katie, Matthew, and Peter visited Grandma for a group overnighter. Grandma liked to say it was a time "for children only!"

"Are we going to do all the same things we do every birthday?" asked Matthew, as the children gathered inside.

"Of course!" replied Grandma. "We have our own special traditions, don't we?"

"What's a tradition?" Peter wanted to know.

"I know! I know!" answered Matthew. "You do the same fun things every year."

"Exactly! And tonight we'll start another new tradition," Grandma announced. "It's something we can do every time you visit!"

"What is it?" the three children chimed.

"Come into the kitchen and I'll show you," said Grandma, leading the way.

The children squealed with excitement as

they entered the room. The table was set for dinner with Grandma's gleaming white china. Eight colorful candles (in honor of Peter) flickered festively in the table's center. And right on top of each plate was a present wrapped in glittery gold paper!

"There's one for each of us!" Matthew exclaimed. "Can we open them now, Grandma?" he asked, his face full of anticipation.

"A book!" said Katie, unwrapping hers. She opened the book's cover. On the first page, written in Grandma's beautiful, artistic penmanship, she read:

> *Believe in the wonder,*
> *Believe if you dare,*
> *Believe in your heart,*
> *Just believe . . . and you're there!*

"Believe and you're *there*? Where's *there*?" Peter asked.

Grandma looked at each of her grandchildren in turn. Then, with her voice full of meaning and mystery, she replied slowly, "That is something I hope you'll discover."

"Okay!" said Katie excitedly, and she turned the page, expecting to find the answer to Peter's question. But her hope turned quickly to disappointment and confusion. "There's nothing else written in mine, Grandma," she said.

"Mine's blank, too!" echoed Matthew.

Grandma nodded. "That's right. There is nothing written in any of them. These books are journals. It's your job to fill your journal with words and pictures. You're the authors!"

Grandma continued, "Because Peter is turning eight this year, and he will soon get baptized, I thought it would be fun for all of us to record in our journals how we felt when we were baptized. How does that sound?"

Peter blurted out, "I just hope we're going to eat first because I'm starving!"

"Of course, children," laughed Grandma. "We're getting ahead of ourselves, aren't we? Let's eat, and then we'll get on with our traditions."

Everyone went to work, and in no time dinner was on the table, eaten, and cleaned up. Then came the moment they'd been waiting for.

"Grandma, we're ready!" the children cried

with one voice, jumping up and down impatiently.

"All right, my darlings. The time has come!" Grandma declared importantly. "Let's all go out to the cottage!"

Chapter Two

A Special Painting

"Hooray!" shouted the children. "The cottage! Hooray!"

A visit to the cottage was always the highlight of a weekend with Grandma. Grandma was an artist, and inside the small building in her backyard she created the most wonderful paintings in the whole world. (At least her three grandchildren thought so!)

"Do you have your journals?" asked Grandma.

"Yes!" they all replied, holding up their new books.

"Then who's leading the way?" she asked

"I am!" shouted Peter, shooting his hand into the air. "Everyone line up!"

The children tromped out the door and along the flagstone path. They hurried across the lawn, past the garden, and through the pine trees. And there it was! Nestled in the corner of the yard stood a little white building with an arched blue door. Cheerful flower baskets dripping with colorful blossoms hung from the eaves. Gentle puffs of smoke rose above the chimney, and every window was radiant with golden warmth from the fire Grandma had already prepared.

Peering in through a window, Katie turned to Grandma, beaming. "I knew it! You've finished another painting! I was hoping you would."

Returning her smile, Grandma replied, "I did, Katie. I painted a new picture. But this one is extra special. I painted it to help make Peter's baptism more meaningful to him." She paused. "And to all of us," she added.

The boys rushed to the window, cupping their hands around their eyes, to see the painting.

Chuckling, Grandma unlocked the blue door. "Why don't we go inside and get a better look?"

she said. But she hesitated before turning the door-knob, looking thoughtful.

"What are we waiting for?" Peter asked, dancing from one impatient foot to the other.

"I'm thinking we should have a special pass-word," Grandma mused aloud.

"How about 'Open Sesame!'" Peter suggested.

Grandma laughed, "Well, I don't know. Our trips to the cottage are pretty special . . ."

"I have an idea," Katie offered, clutching her journal.

"Ah-hah! I bet I know what it is," Matthew replied.

Together they opened their journals and read from the first page.

> Believe in the wonder,
> Believe if you dare,
> Believe in your heart,
> Just believe . . . and you're there!

"That's a great password," Peter agreed heartily.

"Katie, you take the first line," Grandma proposed. "Matthew, the second . . ."

"I'll take the third!" Peter cried.

"And we'll all join in on the last one!" Grandma finished, grinning her approval. "Katie, you lead out."

"Believe in the wonder," she said, turning to Matthew.

Matthew continued, "Believe if you dare."

"Believe in your heart," Peter added.

"Just believe . . . and you're there!" they finished in unison.

Grandma stood aside and, with a flourish, threw open the door of the cottage.

Once inside, the children headed straight for the painting. Unlike the many canvasses strewn about the cottage that still needed work, this painting was completely finished and framed in beautifully carved wood. It was displayed on a large easel near the fireplace.

"That looks like it's in another country," Matthew observed, looking at a river winding through a green landscape. Small groups of people were making their way along a narrow footpath toward a man standing at the river's edge. He was facing a large crowd of people seated on a hillside that sloped down to the water.

"You're right! It's a place far away from here—a place we're going to read about tonight in the scriptures," said Grandma. "This is a painting of Palestine, the place where Jesus lived."

"What river is that?" asked Matthew.

"Could it be the River Jordan?" asked Katie. "That's the only river over there I've ever heard of."

"The River Jordan?" Peter was thinking out loud. "I remember! That's where Jesus was baptized. Hey, just like me! I'm going to be baptized, too."

"You sure are!" Grandma said brightly. "Do you feel ready to be baptized, honey?"

"What do you have to do to be ready?" Peter sounded puzzled.

"You don't know what you have to do?" Matthew was surprised.

Katie encouraged Peter, "I'm sure you know some of the things, don't you?"

"You mean like doing all the right things all the time?" he ventured.

Grandma laughed. "If you can do that, honey,

you're a lot better than the rest of us. But that's the right idea. Obeying the commandments is a very good start."

"You have to repent, too," offered Matthew. "That means being sorry for the wrong things you've done and then asking for forgiveness."

"Yes, Matthew. Repentance is another important step before baptism," Grandma agreed. "Then your sins are washed away."

"But Jesus didn't have any sins," interjected Katie. "Why did He get baptized?"

"Good question, Katie," said Grandma. "Come sit down." On the floor in front of the painting and near the warm fire, Grandma had laid out big pillows and soft blankets.

She pointed to the painting. "Now the man standing before all these people at the river is John the Baptist," Grandma began. "He is teaching them the things they should do in order to be baptized. I'll start reading the story, and I think you'll discover the answer to your question, Katie. Everyone settle back, get comfortable, and pretend that you're there."

She picked up her scriptures and began. "In

those days came John the Baptist, preaching in the wilderness of Judea, and saying, Repent ye: for the kingdom of heaven is at hand."

As Grandma read, Katie imagined people journeying through the wilderness to be baptized. Trying to get the picture in her mind, she looked at Grandma's painting of the river and the prophet John. It all seemed so real that she thought for a moment that she could actually hear the water gurgling. She looked closer . . . the current looked as though it was moving! Could it be?

She looked around to see if the others had noticed, but Grandma was still reading, and the boys were listening carefully. Silently, Katie motioned to Matthew and Peter. Putting a finger to her lips to keep them quiet, she pointed to the river. Drawing close to the painting, they all saw the same thing: The river shimmered as it flowed in the late afternoon sun . . . and the people in the painting were actually moving toward John the Baptist! Dumbfounded, the children looked at each other with their mouths hanging open.

Then Matthew, who was always the most curious of the bunch, couldn't resist any longer. Slowly,

he reached up to touch the painting, and to his amazement, his finger disappeared right into the river! Startled, he yanked it out . . . and water splashed on him as he did! Katie clapped her hand over her mouth to stifle a squeal of surprise.

Not wanting to be left out of the fun, impulsive Peter plunged his whole hand into the painting. But his arm kept going! First his wrist vanished, then his elbow, and then his upper arm. Matthew grabbed Peter's free hand (before he was entirely swallowed up!) and then instinctively reached out for Katie with his other hand.

The moment the children's hands connected, Grandma's voice began to fade. With hands clasped together, all three children felt themselves lifted up and drawn forward. They were being pulled right into the landscape of Grandma's painting!

Chapter Three

On the Banks of the River Jordan

"Whoa-a-a," breathed Matthew, as he felt the rush of air around him. Frightened for a moment, he squeezed his eyes shut. Then, gathering courage, he slowly opened them again.

"Hey, we're headed right for the river in the painting!"" he said. Looking over at fearless Peter, Matthew saw that his little brother's eyes were wide and smiling.

"Look at us!" shouted Peter gleefully. "We're flying!"

"Not exactly," said practical Katie, "because we're not doing anything to make it happen."

The children looked at one another in wonder. "I don't know what's happening," said Matthew, "but we're definitely in for an adventure."

"We're going down!" cried Peter. "I think we're going to land or . . . or whatever you want to call it!" Before he could finish his words, the three children felt their feet softly touch the ground in an opening right in the middle of a thicket of short, scraggly trees near the river's edge. Grandma and her cottage were nowhere to be seen.

Suddenly, Peter began laughing his deep belly laugh. "Matthew, look at you! Where did you get those funny clothes?" Matthew looked down and discovered he was no longer wearing jeans and a T-shirt. Draped across his shoulders were large, loose scarves of grey and brown that reached to his knees. They were cinched at the waist with a piece of braided rope—just like on the people they had seen in Grandma's painting.

Looking Peter up and down, Matthew replied with a smirk, "I wouldn't be laughing if I were you. Look at yourself!"

"We're all looking pretty funny," Katie observed

as she examined her own new outfit. "But if we're really in Grandma's picture, at least we'll fit in!"

When Katie finished talking and the children were silent for a moment, they heard voices nearby. Shoulder to shoulder, they cautiously crept through the trees and peered out of the grove.

Not far away was the trail that led to the river. A stream of people were following it down to the water's edge, just a stone's throw away. There, dozens of people were seated on the gently sloping banks, which formed a natural theater from which to observe. Farther down the river, donkeys were tied to trees and shrubs, quietly resting.

As the children surveyed the scene, Peter (who loved all animals) challenged Matthew, "I'll race you to the donkeys!" And in a flash, both boys were running headlong toward the animals.

"Not so fast," called Katie, hurrying to join them.

When she caught up, breathless Katie reminded her little brothers, "Settle down, boys. We don't belong here, you know. I think we'd better try to fit in."

"Right, Sis," Matthew agreed. "I guess we did get a little excited, didn't we?"

Closer to the river now, the children could hear a man speaking loudly to the seated crowd. "Hey, that must be John the Baptist," Katie said softly. "I'll bet he's teaching all these people about baptism."

"What are those funny clothes he has on?" Peter asked.

"They look like some kind of animal skins to me," Matthew said. "Let's get a closer look." The three children made their way down the embankment toward the river and found an empty spot to sit.

"Repent ye: for the kingdom of heaven is at hand," John spoke with reverent feeling. "I indeed baptize you with water unto repentance: but he that cometh after me is mightier than I, whose shoes I am not worthy to bear: he shall baptize you with the Holy Ghost, and with fire."

As John was speaking, Katie looked around at the people who had come to listen. Many were with families, some sat alone, some were old, and some were very young. All seemed completely absorbed in John's teaching.

Katie noticed one family coming to join the group. The father carried a little girl of about seven, as a boy who looked to be Katie's age led them through the crowd. There was no mother with them.

"This seems like a good spot, Father," the boy said, pointing to an open space next to Matthew, Katie, and Peter.

"Yes, it does," the father replied. "Could you

spread the blanket so that Abigail will have a comfortable place to sit?" he asked his son.

The boy tried to remove the blanket draped over his shoulder, but it was caught behind him in the strap of his leather satchel. The harder he pulled, the worse the problem became. Just when it seemed that the blanket might strangle him, Katie, who couldn't help smiling at the boy's predicament, calmly walked over to rescue him.

"It looks like you could use a little help with that blanket," she offered.

"No, really, I can get it," he insisted as he tugged.

But he only succeeded at tightening the tangle. Katie tried again. "You might as well let me help you. I can see just what the problem is."

"Well, if you really want to," the exasperated boy said with a shrug.

Smiling at him, Katie untangled the blanket from the strap. "There you go," she said, trying not to look smug.

"Thanks," replied the boy, looking a bit sheepish. "My name is Jesse."

"I'm Katherine Claire, but everyone just calls me Katie," she responded.

"Katie. That is a name I've never heard before. I like it!" Jesse declared, as he spread the blanket on the ground.

As Jesse's father gently placed the young girl on the blanket, Katie noticed that her legs were thin and limp. It seemed they couldn't move at all.

But before Katie could talk to the girl, Jesse's father said, "I see you have made a friend, son."

"Yes, Father," Jesse answered. "This is Katie. She helped me with the blanket."

"I noticed that." The man winked at Katie. "I am Seth, and this is my daughter, Abigail."

Abigail beamed at Katie and said eagerly, "I am very glad to meet you, Katie! Have you come from Jerusalem to hear John preach?"

"Uh . . . umm . . . we came from a little farther away than that," Katie stammered, "but we did come to hear John preach. Where do *you* come from?" she quickly asked, trying to shift the attention from herself.

"We are from Galilee," Seth answered. "I have business to conduct in Jerusalem. As we traveled, we heard that John the Baptist was preaching here at the River Jordan. My grandfather knew his father many years ago, and so we decided to make the day's journey to hear him." Then, looking around, Seth asked, "Are your parents nearby, Katie?"

"Well . . . uh . . . my parents . . . um . . . couldn't be here. I came with my two brothers." Katie beckoned to Matthew and Peter to come over. "Matthew and Peter, come meet some new friends."

Peter, always ready to make friends, quickly crawled over. "Hi, I'm Peter, and this is my brother, Matthew." Matthew waved his hello.

"I'm Jesse, this is my father, Seth, and sitting right there is my sister, Abigail," Jesse introduced his family.

"Hi, Abigail." Peter warmed to the little girl who seemed about his age. "Do you want to come with us to listen from that rock over there?" he invited her.

"I would like to go, but I cannot walk on my own," Abigail responded matter-of-factly. "I'm a paralytic."

"A what?" Peter questioned.

"A paralytic. That means my legs do not work," she calmly explained. "Someone has to carry me wherever I go."

"That's awful!" Peter moaned. He couldn't imagine not being able to run about freely.

"I'm used to it," Abigail reassured Peter. "I have been this way all my life."

"Hey, I've got an idea!" Peter was excited. "Matthew, come over here. Let's make a chair with our arms to carry Abigail. Then we can all sit together."

Katie and Jesse watched as the two brothers tenderly carried Abigail between them and set her gently on the rock. Then, they climbed up on either side of her protectively, and the three of them sat happily together, listening to John the Baptist preach.

Chapter Four

Facing the Pharisees

Suddenly, the sound of John's voice was drowned out by a group of noisy men making their way down the hillside, talking loudly to each other as they walked. They appeared very different from most of the people who had come to hear John. Dressed in rich robes of flowing red and gold silk that swished as they walked, they raised their heads and their voices as if they were royalty. Adding to their appearance of superiority were gold bracelets adorning their wrists and rings crusted with rubies and other precious stones on every finger.

The two leaders of the group looked around

disdainfully at the believers gathered on the bank of the river. Not caring that others were trying to hear John's sermon, one said to the other, "Azor, I dislike being among these common people. I feel *filthy* just being here."

The man named Azor nodded in agreement, his mouth twisted into a sneer. "I do too, Erastus. Let us get the information we need at once so we can return to Jerusalem and make our report to the Council."

"Yes, we shall act quickly," Erastus replied.

"Who are those men?" Matthew asked Abigail.

"You don't know who the Pharisees are?" Abigail responded in disbelief. "They are very religious men who study the law of Moses in the scriptures. They pride themselves on following every rule exactly."

"And they keep themselves separate from everyone else," Jesse added from his seat nearby, "because they believe that ordinary people like us are wicked and unworthy."

But before Matthew could ask more, John raised his voice above the sound of the Pharisees. Now standing waist-deep in the water, he called out, "Repent ye: for the kingdom of heaven is at hand."

"Look at him! He looks like a wild man," laughed one of the Pharisees scornfully. "His clothes are made of camel skins."

Another responded with a smirk, "Does he really think he has the authority to preach to *us*?"

"Blasphemous!" exclaimed the Pharisee called Azor. "This man has not been properly tutored in the law!"

"Of course not," interjected Erastus. "I hear he has lived in the desert most of his life. What could *he* know of the scriptural law?"

"Perhaps those Pharisees don't know who John's parents were," commented Seth to Katie and Jesse, who were seated with him on the blanket. "I think they'd be interested to know."

Seth stood and approached the men. "Forgive me," he began, "I have been listening to your discussion."

"Who are you?" Erastus demanded.

"I am Seth bar Lamethus. I am from the same village where John was born. He left as a baby, so I don't know him personally, but both of his parents were of priestly descent. I know his father served in the temple," Seth explained.

"What is that to us?" challenged Azor. "It makes not a whit of difference. Maybe his father was a priest, but this man is a heathen!"

Drawing near to Seth, Erastus narrowed his eyes and asked, "Do you agree with this Baptist man?"

"I just arrived. I have not yet heard enough to—" Seth began.

The haughty Pharisee cut him off angrily. "You have not heard enough? Surely it is obvious to you that this 'prophet' doesn't know what he is talking about. You are not a Pharisee, I take it?"

"No, I am not," Seth confirmed. "I am a publican."

"You're a *tax collector*?" Erastus threw back his head and laughed a loud, arrogant laugh. "I have spent a lifetime studying the law, and a *tax collector* is trying to tell me what is what! *Ha!*"

Pushing Seth aside, Azor summoned all the Pharisees. "Come! We must waste no more time talking to this sinner!" And with that, the men rustled their robes pompously, their heavy jewelry clanking as they strode through the seated crowd toward the river's edge.

Once gathered on the banks, the Pharisees began taunting the humble prophet standing in the water.

"Who are you?" Azor demanded. "Do you think you are the Christ?"

"I am not the Christ," answered John, clearly and calmly.

"What then? Are you Elias the prophet?" Erastus challenged.

"I am not." Again, John seemed unshaken.

"Who art thou that we may give an answer to them that sent us?" Azor asked.

"I am the voice of one crying in the wilderness," John replied. "Bring ye forth fruits meet for repentance."

This outraged the Pharisees. Didn't John know how learned and holy they were? One shouted at John, "Surely you know that we are the posterity of Abraham, and we have our place assured in the kingdom of God. How dare you tell *us* to repent!"

But John did not shrink. "Think not to say within yourselves, We have Abraham to our father:

For I say unto you, that God is able of these stones to raise up children unto Abraham."

Fuming, Azor barked defiantly, "You're nobody! You said yourself that you are not Elias nor the Christ. What makes you think you can baptize?"

With quiet strength, John answered, "I indeed baptize you with water unto repentance: but he that cometh after me is mightier than I, whose shoes I am not worthy to bear: He shall baptize you with the Holy Ghost, and with fire."

Azor, infuriated by John's refusal to be swayed, turned to the other Pharisees, "Come, we have heard enough. The Council will be very interested indeed in what has gone on here. Let us leave this place now so we will not become polluted by these teachings."

"Why don't the Pharisees like John?" Matthew asked Seth.

Seth sighed. "They consider themselves the only ones who can interpret and uphold the law."

"But John is only trying to tell them about repentance and baptism," Katie pointed out.

"That's the problem. They do not want anybody telling them what they should do or how they should do it," Jesse replied.

"But don't they want to know the truth?" asked Peter.

"They only want to know their own truth," Jesse said sadly, as the Pharisees noisily mounted their horses and galloped away, their robes whipping in the wind behind them.

Chapter Five

"Be Still, Everyone!"

"Father," called Abigail from the rock where she had been sitting. "This rock is getting very hard. Could you help me down?"

"Oh, Abigail, you *have* been sitting there a long time, haven't you?" Seth sounded apologetic. "Thank you for being patient while I was speaking with those proud Pharisees. If the law of Moses makes people act like they do, I am not sure I want to follow it!"

With that, he bent down to pick up his daughter. She slipped her arms around his neck, and they started down the path that led to the donkeys.

Falling in right behind, Jesse motioned for his new friends to follow.

"Where are we going?" Katie asked Matthew, as he marched ahead confidently.

"Uh . . . I . . . I guess I'm following them," said Matthew, not sounding as confident as he looked.

"I can see that." Katie sounded exasperated as she asked, "But where are *they* going?"

"I'll go ask!" Peter offered.

"Wait!" Katie implored, but she was too late. Peter was already out of earshot, springing happily up the hill. Katie sighed.

"What's wrong, Sis?" asked Matthew gently. "You seem stressed out."

"Well, for one thing, how long are we going to be here?" Katie began. "For another, where are we going to sleep tonight? And what happens when Peter gets hungry? And the most important thing: How are we supposed to get back home?"

Matthew's mind was racing. He hated to admit it, but Katie had asked some awfully good questions. As he was trying to come up with at least one good answer, Peter reappeared on the scene. "Hey, I've got good news!" he announced. "Seth invited us to stay with them tonight. He asked me where our parents were, and I told him that they were at our home, far away. When I said I didn't think we could make it back home before nightfall, he said we could bed down at their campfire! Come on!"

Katie and Matthew, relieved that at least they had a place to sleep, followed Peter past several other campfires to the place where Seth and Jesse were preparing to camp for the night.

"Hello!" Seth welcomed them warmly. "We are glad you have come. We have only a simple meal, but at least it will fill our bellies. Boys, would you collect some firewood?"

"Yeah! Let's go," shouted Peter, running in the direction of some trees.

Watching him take off, Jesse asked laughingly, "Does he run everywhere he goes?"

"Pretty much," Matthew answered. "You've got to be on your toes to keep up with him."

"Well, we should hurry then," replied Jesse as he started running too, "or we will surely be left behind."

At the campsite, Katie helped Abigail prepare

the supper. Abigail pulled some small wooden bowls from a basket Seth had placed at her side. Then she said, "Katie, there is a sack hanging over the donkey. Would you get it for me?"

"Sure," Katie tried to sound casual. She wasn't used to large animals, and she certainly hadn't ever been near a donkey, but she was determined not to let Abigail see her fear.

"Okay, boy," she talked to the donkey under her breath as she approached. "I'm just going to lift this sack off your back. That's right . . . hold still there . . . good boy . . . all done." And as quick as she could, Katie ran back to where Abigail was seated.

As Abigail and Katie broke a large loaf of bread into pieces and distributed almonds, dates, and cheese into the bowls, Peter came huffing and puffing into the camp, dragging a tree branch nearly twice his size.

"Well, that is a lot of wood for such a small fellow!" Seth said with admiration. "I shall start breaking it into smaller pieces."

Jesse and Matthew laid some twigs for kindling, and Seth added some larger sticks from Peter's branch. The boys watched as Seth expertly lit the kindling with his flint and the campfire burst into a warm and steady flame.

With perfect timing, Abigail announced from her blanket, "Supper is ready! Let us eat!"

As everyone sat on the blankets, Jesse asked, "Father, could we offer thanks for this food, our warm fire, and our new friends?"

"Of course," Seth replied, and he turned to the other children, smiling. "It is a lucky man who is taught by his son." Then he explained, "Just one year ago, my wife died of the fever. We all miss her terribly, and I have not felt much like praying since then. But my children still believe, and Jesse always reminds us to thank God before we eat."

"I am sorry about your mother," Katie whispered to Abigail as they bowed their heads. In reply, Abigail squeezed Katie's hand gratefully, and held on tight all through Jesse's fervent prayer.

As Jesse concluded, a frantic commotion was heard from some nearby campfires. Several voices called out in loud alarm, "Wild boars! Wild boars coming!"

Katie had read about boars. They were vicious,

wild pigs that were quicker than humans. Terrified at the thought, she started to scramble to her feet, ready to run. But Abigail grabbed her hand and yanked her back down. Seth dove for Matthew and Peter, gripping their shoulders to keep them close to the ground.

"Be still, everyone!" he commanded in a loud, raspy whisper. "They will only chase us if we run. And I promise you, they are faster than we are."

Just then, a small brown gopher tore through their camp in a flurry. It ran right over Abigail's still

foot, and Katie, forgetting her fear, instinctively grabbed the crippled leg, pulling it close to Abigail's body. She was just in the nick of time, for right behind the gopher came three snarling pigs in hot pursuit.

"Nobody move," Seth cautioned, his voice tight and panicky. All the children froze as the boars charged through camp, just missing Abigail and Katie who were huddled together. On the trail of the gopher, the wild boars stampeded, their

mouths opened wide, ready to devour anything that resembled food.

No one dared breathe until the sound of thundering feet began to subside as the hapless gopher led the chase up a nearby hill—with the hungry boars right behind.

Chapter Six

The Birth of a Baptist

"The danger is past, children." Seth stood up. He went right to Katie, who was still seated. Kneeling down, he said gratefully, "Thank you for moving Abigail's foot. Surely the boars would have trampled it if you hadn't taken such quick action. You are a brave and kind girl." Seth put his arm around Katie's shoulder and gave her a warm squeeze.

Then he helped Abigail get situated again, smoothing the blanket around her. "Will the boars be back, Father?" Abigail asked, her voice still trembling from the scare.

"No," said Seth, imagining the sad plight of the gopher. "Now they are fed, and they'll head back to their burrow. We won't see them again tonight. Come close to the fire, children, and we'll eat."

The children sat shoulder to shoulder, feeling protection in the closeness. Gradually, they felt their fear leave, and they began to share the meager supper.

While the others ate eagerly, Matthew asked Seth about John the Baptist. "You said John was born in your village, right? Did you know him? Was he your friend?"

"Not really," replied Seth, chewing his almonds thoughtfully. "He is younger than I, and his parents were much older than mine. In fact, John's father was a friend to my grandfather."

"Father, tell what happened in the temple, ple-e-ease?!" begged Abigail.

"Oh, yes, Father!" Jesse echoed. "I love that story!"

"All right, my angels," said Seth kindly. And he began.

"John's father, Zacharias, was very old. So was his wife, Elisabeth. They had prayed to have a child for years, but it had not happened. Then they became as old as grandparents—much too old to have a baby. At least that's what we all thought.

"Now, every spring and fall, Zacharias went to Jerusalem to serve in the temple for a week. He was a priest, you see. One day, he was chosen to burn incense at the altar. This was a great honor, and he had never been chosen before.

"Well, as he knelt to do this special job, an angel appeared at the right side of the altar."

"An angel? A real angel with wings?" Peter interrupted. "Scary!"

"Well," Seth chuckled, "I do not think he had wings, but he was a real angel, all right. And Zacharias was definitely scared. Then the angel said, 'Fear not, Zacharias. For thy prayer is heard; and thy wife Elisabeth shall bear thee a son and thou shalt call his name John.'"

"She was going to have a baby, even though she was as old as a grandma?" asked wide-eyed Peter. "I don't believe it!"

"Well," Seth replied, "neither did old Zacharias. He said to the angel, 'whereby shall I know this?

For I am an old man, and my wife is well stricken in years.'"

"He said that? To the angel?" Katie asked.

"He did indeed!" Seth replied. "And the angel answered Zacharias this way: 'Behold, thou shalt be dumb, and not able to speak, until the day these things shall be performed, because thou believest not my words, which shall be fulfilled.'"

"So he couldn't talk at all?" Matthew asked.

Seth shook his head. "Not a word. Zacharias had to use a writing tablet to communicate."

"Man, he should have just believed the angel in the first place!" exclaimed Peter.

"Yes, I suppose he should have," Seth agreed. "But, after the baby was born and everyone thought he should be named Zacharias after his father, Zacharias shook his head and wrote on the tablet, 'His name is John.' And immediately after he wrote those words, his voice returned."

"Wow! John must have been one special baby," Peter said in awe.

"It sure seemed that way," Seth nodded. "In fact, after he could talk again, Zacharias prophesied about John. He said, 'Thou, child, shalt be called the prophet of the Highest; for thou shalt go before the face of the Lord to prepare his ways.'"

Seth continued, "My father and grandfather always said that John was born to bring us God's message. I guess that's why we have come. When my children heard he was preaching, they wanted to hear what he had to say. I guess I did, too."

"Father, today when I heard John prophesy that someone is coming who is even greater than he is, my heart told me that it will be the Messiah," Jesse said.

"Jesse, you have your mother's heart," Seth said tenderly. "A believing heart."

"I believe, too, Father," Abigail said, her eyes shining with faith. "I believe John is the special prophet sent to prepare us for the Lord's coming."

"Yes, Father, and when He comes, I believe He will heal Abigail," Jesse added in a determined voice.

"Perhaps," said Seth doubtfully, "but we must learn to be happy with what we are given."

Abigail looked into her father's eyes and said, "I am happy, Father. I am *very* happy. But I am happiest when I trust in God's word."

"And a little child shall lead them," Seth said softly, smiling lovingly at his faithful children. "Perhaps you two are right. Perhaps John is a prophet, but I will have to hear more to be convinced for myself."

"I'm with Jesse and Abigail," Peter piped up from across the campfire. Matthew and Katie nodded in agreement.

"I'm surrounded by believers," Seth laughed. Then, yawning, he said, "Morning will come all too soon, children. It is time for sleep."

"I want to sleep by Katie," Abigail declared. "Come, share my blanket, Katie."

"I would like that," said Katie, lying down next to her new friend. "We can pretend we're sisters."

"Boys, you can sleep over here," Seth said, motioning to some blankets and animal skins he had spread on the ground.

"This is better than any sleepover," Peter whispered in Matthew's ear. "I'll bet this is what it feels like to be a Boy Scout!"

"This is fun, all right," Matthew replied. But inside, he wondered how they were ever going to get home.

Jesse lay on the animal skins next to the two brothers, humming softly to himself.

"What are you humming?" Matthew asked him.

"It is a song that was a favorite of our mother's. I sing it to Abigail when she cannot sleep. Would you like to hear it?" Jesse offered.

"Please," responded Matthew gratefully. "We would love it." And Matthew and Peter settled into their strange beds as Jesse's clear voice rang out in the darkness:

> *When hearts are sad and all our burdens*
> *Heavy on us weigh,*
> *When death and pain come visit us*
> *And grief seems here to stay.*
> *We hear the voice of prophets, raised*
> *To us in days gone by:*
> *"The Lord is coming to the earth,*
> *The time is drawing nigh."*
> *Then sing to Him, our loving Lord,*
> *Messiah, Savior, King.*
> *Come, fill our grieving hearts with hope,*
> *And sweet salvation bring.*

Messiah, come with healing wings,
Our sorrows to defeat.
Messiah, turn all strife to love,
And make our joy complete.

Lying alone next to the fire, Seth listened to his son singing and thought about the promised Messiah. *Is He really coming? Could He really heal my Abigail? Could He ever bring true peace to my troubled heart?*

If only, thought Seth, *if only I, too, could believe.*

Chapter Seven

A Family Wounded

A ray of sunlight beamed over the rocks, alighting on sleeping Peter's face. Awakening with a start, he sat up on his blanket, trying to remember just where he was.

"Hey, I camped out last night!" he exclaimed. "Cool! Really cool!"

"It doesn't feel cool out here to me," said Jesse, now stirring. "The sun is already hot as noonday!" He looked at Peter as though he must be crazy.

"You're right, Jesse," Matthew said hastily, rubbing his eyes. "Peter, you must have meant to say 'Really hot!'" Matthew gave Peter a meaningful wink.

"Oh, right," said Peter, catching on. "I guess I wasn't awake all the way."

"Let us roll up our blankets and leave them here while we go down to the river," Seth suggested.

Peter rolled up his in no time. "Wow! It sure would be great if we could make *our* beds this fast every morning," he said quietly to Katie.

"I think you could make yours a whole lot faster if you didn't spend so much time complaining," Katie teased her little brother.

"I hate to admit it, but you're probably right," Peter grudgingly agreed.

Eager to hear John continue preaching, Jesse enlisted Matthew's help to carry Abigail down to the river. "Matthew, let us make a chair like you and Peter did yesterday."

"Great idea! Here we go, Abigail," said Matthew, and he and Jesse hoisted her up as if she were on a throne. She put her arms gratefully around their necks and off they went, Katie and Peter walking right alongside them as Seth brought up the rear.

The crowd became more dense as they approached the banks of the river. Seth looked around for a comfortable place to sit. It was warm

already, and the prime spots in the shade were quickly being taken. He spied a clearing ahead of them shielded by a broad, leafy tree. "Excuse me." He approached a man who was seated with his family in a portion of the shade. "Is there room here for my family, too?"

The man's eyes narrowed as he saw Seth, and he replied gruffly, "There's no room here for a publican. No room at all."

Taken aback, Katie quietly asked Jesse, "Why is that man being rude to your father?"

"Because Father is a publican," Jessie answered.

"A publican?" Matthew questioned.

Jesse, hanging his head as if he were a little embarrassed, explained, "A publican is someone who collects taxes."

"Doesn't *someone* have to collect them?" Matthew inquired.

"Yes, I guess someone does," Jesse acknowledged. "But publicans get paid by charging people more than the Romans require. That is how my father makes a living. Many publicans get rich by charging lots of extra money. But my father does not do that."

Seth, surprised by the man's anger, asked him, "Do I know you? Why do you speak to me so?"

"I guess you cannot remember all of the people you steal from," the man replied bitterly.

"I do not steal from people," Seth insisted.

"I call it stealing when a publican invades a home, demands money that the family cannot spare, and then keeps some for himself," the man countered, shaking his pointing finger at Seth.

"Sir, I am a publican, but believe me, I do not demand—" Seth tried to explain.

The man interrupted. "I am Joel bar Daniel, and this is my family," he said, gesturing to his wife and the three small children peeking out from behind her skirts. "When you came to our house to collect taxes, I told you we would have no money left if you took all that you demanded. But you said I had to pay the tax or face the Roman guard. Imagine how I felt when I had to tell my wife that there was not enough money to buy food. My children went hungry for weeks." The man's voice quavered with anger as he spoke.

"Well, my children have to eat, too," Seth argued, his voice now strident and harsh.

"But it is at the expense of others," the man named Joel insisted.

"You should be glad that I do not ask for as much money as most tax collectors," Seth retorted. "I try to be as fair as I can."

"I do not believe you," Joel was almost shouting now. "A publican is a thief! And you come here to be baptized? Shame! Shame!"

"I have not come to be baptized." Seth's voice was quiet now, his eyes downcast. "I am here because my children wanted to come."

"Well, maybe they can teach you a lesson or two about being an honest person. Come!" Joel instructed his family. "Gather up our things. It is better for us to sit in the sun than to be near this man."

Joel's family hurriedly picked up their blankets and baskets and with disgust written all over their faces, they made their way across the hillside, looking for another shady place to sit.

Chapter Eight

A Change of Heart

Seth felt the stares of many in the crowd as he watched Joel and his family disappear into the gathering multitude. He tried to look as if he didn't care about Joel's accusations, but inside, Seth felt the sting of his words. Forcing a smile, he sat down with his children and busied himself arranging the blankets.

"Father," Jesse asked him quietly, "does that man speak the truth?"

"Do not worry about it now, son. John has started to preach," Seth reassured Jesse. "We can talk later."

Jesse looked around the hillside and noticed that, once again, the Pharisees had gathered. They stood in groups, laughing loudly, as if to say that John's teachings didn't apply to them. Then John's voice became stronger and more piercing, and he seemed to speak right to the mocking Pharisees.

"The axe is laid unto the root of the trees," he declared. "Every tree therefore which bringeth not forth good fruit is hewn down, and cast into the fire."

"What does he mean by that?" Matthew asked Jesse.

"I think he means that if we do not do the right things, we will be cut off from God, and maybe even destroyed," Jesse replied.

At this warning, many in the crowd earnestly called out to John, "What shall we do then? What shall we do?"

And John answered them with fervent feeling, "He that hath two coats, let him impart to him that hath none; and he that hath meat, let him do likewise."

Jesse turned to his father and said, "He is

saying that we should be generous with one another, isn't he?"

"Yes, Jesse," Seth replied, "I think that is exactly what he is saying."

Then Jesse said haltingly, "Perhaps that is why that man named Joel was unhappy with you. He thinks you wanted to keep some money for yourself." Jesse could hardly look at his father as he spoke.

"Perhaps I did," Seth replied softly. "Maybe I did." And it seemed he was thinking aloud as he spoke.

Just then a group of men approached the river, saying to John that they wished to be baptized. Seth sat upright, an astonished look coming over his face. "What is it, Father?" Jesse asked.

"I know those men," Seth replied. "They are publicans, just like I am."

Then, humbly and in pleading tones, the men asked John, "Master, what shall we do?"

With conviction and perfect clarity, John answered the hopeful men, "Exact no more than that which is appointed you."

Sensing that something important had been said,

Peter whispered to Katie, "What does it mean to 'exact no more than that which is appointed you'?"

Katie whispered back, "It means that those tax collectors should only take as much as required. They shouldn't take extra money for themselves."

Meanwhile, Seth sat perfectly still, feeling as though a thunderbolt had struck his heart. He thought of his confrontation with Joel only a short time before. It was true that he did not exact as much as most publicans, but that didn't make his actions right. He had sometimes taken more money than he had to. And he knew it.

The faces of Joel's wife and children burned in his mind. *How could I have let myself become such a person?* he asked himself silently. *I thought I was a kind person, yet I caused this family pain. I thought I was an honest man, yet I have taken more money from people than was rightfully mine.*

Then Seth was overcome with sadness. Sadness for his sins, sadness for those he had wronged, sadness for his motherless children, and sadness that his Rebecca was no longer here to help him figure out what he should do now.

Just then, some Roman soldiers went to the riverbank and spoke to John, who was standing waist deep in the water where he had been baptizing. They, too, demanded of him, "And what shall *we* do?"

Firmly, John replied, "Do violence to no man, neither accuse any falsely, and be content with your wages."

Some soldiers walked away, apparently unhappy

with John's counsel. But others were touched, promised to change, and asked John to baptize them.

As Seth and the children watched the soldiers emerge one by one from the cleansing water, it appeared that each man had been transformed. Now, instead of looking gruff and combative, each soldier's face radiated joy, light, and peace.

"Oh, Father," Jesse said, "They look so happy, don't they? I did not know that repentance could be such a happy thing!"

"Remarkable, isn't it, son?" Seth said, clearly moved by the soldiers' joy.

"Yes, but . . ." Jesse started.

"What is it, son?" Seth asked.

"It seems impossible to repent of *all* my sins. I have so many. Where do I begin?"

"Take my advice and start now," Seth said soberly. "Do not wait until you are my age."

Then Peter, who had been listening intently, asked, "What happens if you still make mistakes after you're baptized? What then?"

"Repentance really should be a way of life, shouldn't it?" Katie said thoughtfully. "You try not to sin, but when you do, you have to be willing to say you're sorry right away, and not do it again. Isn't that the idea?"

Seth sat in amazement at the things the children understood—things the educated Pharisees didn't seem to get at all! *Sometimes,* he thought, *being an adult gets in the way of listening. Clearly, the children had listened to John as he answered the question "Master, what should we do?"*

And then, an important truth seemed to wash over Seth like warm, cleansing rain: *Listening is just the first step,* he realized. *Actions must follow. That's why so many people asked John, "What should we do?"*

Now Seth knew precisely what *he* had to do. And in that moment, his sadness began to lift, and hope took its place.

"Children, we can talk more later of all we have learned, but now there is something I must do."

Seth arose, and with determination in his step, began making his way across the hill.

"Where is Father going?" asked Abigail.

"He didn't say," Jesse said. "But I have a pretty good idea. Let us follow him and see." Jesse knelt and hoisted Abigail onto his back. "Come on, everyone. Follow me!"

Chapter Nine

The Fruits of Repentance

"That publican is coming this way!" It was Joel speaking to his wife, and he was pointing at Seth as he approached.

Undaunted and full of purpose, Seth came face to face with Joel. Joel stiffened with fear and distrust. But instead of the irritation he felt earlier, now Seth only felt compassion and understanding.

Through an opening in the crowd, Jesse emerged with Abigail on his back, the other three children close behind. They listened as Seth talked to Joel.

"You said some very hard things to me today," Seth began. "Your words still burn in my ears."

"I am glad," Joel retorted. "I do not take any of them back!"

"Neither should you," Seth said. "I have not come to argue or defend myself. I was wrong. As I listened to John today, I knew in my heart what was required of me. I have come to ask your forgiveness for the wrongs I have committed against you and your family."

Joel looked stunned. He turned to his wife and children and then back again to Seth, wondering what to say.

Katie whispered to Jesse, "Your father has a lot of courage. I don't think I could have done that with all these people watching."

Jesse's admiration for his father grew as he watched the scene continue to unfold. "Do you think Joel is going to accept your father's apology?" Matthew asked.

"I hope so," Jesse replied. "I really hope so."

"He still looks kind of mad if you ask me," Peter observed.

The children watched as Seth reached into the

small leather pouch hanging across his chest. He pulled out several gold coins and offered them to Joel. "Please accept this as a—" he began.

"I do not want your money," Joel interrupted Seth, his eyes narrowing with suspicion.

"But this is not my money." Seth looked deep into Joel's eyes as he spoke. "I am only returning what is rightfully yours."

"So you think—?" Joel began bitterly, still unwilling to bend.

But before he could finish, his wife laid her hand softly on his shoulder. "If we truly believe what we have heard these last few days, we must forgive. We are in need of being forgiven ourselves, remember?" she gently entreated her husband.

Joel's anger seemed to soften, but he still stood silent.

"Is he going to do it?" Katie whispered, hardly able to stand the suspense.

"Sometimes it's harder to forgive than to ask forgiveness," Matthew said, "especially when you have been really hurt."

"That is the point of being baptized," said Jesse.

"You let the Lord take away your hurt, so you don't have to carry it anymore."

"I don't think Father believed that when we came here, but I think he is learning it now," Abigail whispered to her brother.

"Yes." Jesse smiled. "Indeed he is."

Joel's wife was still looking at him with pleading eyes that begged him to forgive. Then, Seth broke the silence. "I must make things right, Joel,

or my repentance will not be complete. Please," and he extended the coins farther toward Joel.

Then, slowly, Joel opened his hand. Seth smiled gratefully as he placed the money in the open palm. Joel looked Seth in the eye for a long time and then, suddenly, he grasped Seth's hand firmly in warm friendship.

"You forgive me, then?" Seth asked, his voice filled with emotion.

"Yes, I forgive you," Joel answered sincerely. "I

spoke some unkind words to you earlier today. Will *you* forgive *me?*"

"Of course, but I'll always remember what you said. Because of you, my conscience was pricked when John spoke so boldly to the publicans," Seth explained. "You helped me to repent."

Moved by Seth's penitence, Jesse and the rest of the children instinctively went to his side. Seth embraced Jesse and lifted Abigail from Jesse's back onto his own shoulder.

"This is my daughter, Abigail, and my son, Jesse," he said to Joel. "Children, meet Joel, a very good friend of mine." Seth's voice still trembled with emotion.

"I am glad to meet you, Jesse and Abigail," Joel said.

Then he turned to Seth. "I wanted to be baptized today, my friend. Then after I spoke to you this morning, I felt too angry inside. But now I feel right with the world. Thanks to you, I am ready to go to the river. It would be an honor if you would join me."

"But I—" Seth began.

"That is what you want, isn't it?" Joel asked with a directness that demanded an answer.

Seth paused for a moment, then stammered, "Well, I suppose." He seemed a little surprised by his own answer but then repeated with conviction, "Yes, that is *exactly* what I want."

"Come then, my friend," Joel said warmly, and he put his hand on Seth's shoulder as they descended the riverbank together.

Reaching the river's edge, the two men joined others waiting to be baptized. When it was their turn, John beckoned them to join him in the water. Seth and Joel waded in. Graciously, Joel motioned for Seth to be first.

While Joel beamed his approval, Seth approached John. With the kindest of smiles, the Baptist reached out and grasped Seth's arm. Then looking into Seth's eyes, John spoke with certainty and fervor, "I indeed baptize you unto repentance; but he that cometh after me is mightier than I, whose shoes I am not worthy to bear; he shall baptize you with the Holy Ghost, and with fire."

Seth held onto John's arm as the Baptist lowered him into the river. Immersed in the cool, refreshing water, the noise of the world faded away, and for a moment, Seth felt complete peace. Then, as John raised him up out of the water, the full importance of baptism sank deep into Seth's soul. And in that moment, Seth knew that, indeed, the promised Messiah would come.

Chapter Ten

When the White Dove Descended

Jesse waded out into the water, carrying Abigail on his back, to meet Seth. Seth hugged his children in a long embrace as the water swirled around them.

"Father, I have prayed for this day," Jesse said.

"I have felt your prayers, my son, and longed for my heart to believe as yours does. As your mother's did," Seth spoke frankly to his children. "I did not know how quickly and completely my heart could change."

"All it took was a little faith," Abigail said, smiling happily.

"I didn't stand a chance, did I, with you two praying for me!" Seth replied, laughing, as the three emerged from the water onto the shore.

Katie, Matthew, and Peter met them there. "You look so happy, Seth! I can't wait to be baptized," Peter announced. "I am going to be baptized when I get home, you know."

"Where *is* your home? And who would baptize you *there?*" Jesse asked, thoroughly puzzled. "Is John going to your village . . . ?"

"Oh, my!" Matthew suddenly exclaimed. "Being out in the sun all day is getting to Peter. He hardly knows what he's talking about. You need a little rest, don't you, buddy?" Matthew put his arm around Peter's shoulder and led him behind a nearby rock.

"What's wrong with you?" Matthew asked Peter when they were alone.

"I don't know what you're talking about," Peter insisted. "I'm just fine!"

Matthew voice was pleading, "You've got to think about what you're saying! Right now, in this time, John is the only one who can baptize. It's not

72

like our time, when lots of people have the priest-hood."

"Oh, yeah. Sorry." Peter was starting to see his mistake. "I didn't even think of that."

"If you're not careful," Matthew implored, "you're going to give away our secret, and I don't think anyone would believe our story if we had to tell it. So, let's not talk about your baptism any-more until we get home. Deal?"

"Deal," Peter agreed sheepishly, and the boys headed back to join the others.

"Are you feeling better?" Abigail asked Peter, clearly concerned.

"Yup. Lots better. Thanks." Peter kept his answers short and to the point. He didn't want to make any more blunders.

"Father," Jesse said, "perhaps we should all go back to the camp and get some dry robes for you."

"Good idea . . ." Seth began, but his voice trailed off as a hush fell over the crowd. The chil-dren followed Seth's eyes up the trail. What was everyone looking at?

Then, they saw Him at the top of the grassy bank. He looked like an ordinary man—at least in some ways. Although He was dressed in simple robes, His face was striking in its purity and its power.

Who is this man? Seth was stopped by the man's very presence and found himself unable to move.

Slowly, but with purpose, the man walked past them to the river bank. Sensing something holy about this unusual man, the multitude parted, creating a clear path for Him down to the river.

John stopped preaching and stood silently as the man, strong and serene, walked toward him. It seemed the crowd was hardly breathing as John the Baptist and Jesus of Nazareth came face to face, standing in the River Jordan.

Instinctively, the children, along with many others in the crowd, fell to their knees. Abigail, in her father's arms, whispered in his ear, "Even before I saw Him, I felt something wonderful inside."

"We all did, darling," Seth replied. And then with a wry smile, he added, "even me."

"Not all of us," Matthew corrected, pointing to a group of Pharisees standing apart from the crowd. But even they were silent now.

Seth shook his head and wondered aloud,

"They know the law, but their hearts are far from feeling."

Katie touched Matthew's arm and whispered, "Matthew, the man in the water with John is Jesus, isn't He?"

"Yes, He is, Katie." Matthew's voice was so soft, she could hardly hear him.

John and Jesus were standing together in the water, and John was shaking his head. "I have need to be baptized of thee, and thou comest to me?" he said earnestly to Jesus.

"Who is that man?" Jesse asked his father.

Seth's voice was filled with wonder. "I believe He is the Messiah, son."

"The Messiah? How do you know?" Jesse could hardly believe that the long-awaited Messiah could be here—in the wilderness of Judea!

"From what I feel here," Seth said pointing to his heart. "John said to Him, 'I have need to be baptized of *thee*.' Is there anyone else he would say that to?"

They listened again as Jesus spoke, "Suffer it to be so now. For thus it becometh us to fulfill all righteousness."

"What does He mean?" asked Peter.

"All men on earth need to be baptized to wash away their sins," Katie explained.

"But if He is really the Messiah, He probably has no sins," Abigail said.

"That is right, Abigail," Seth agreed. "But He wants to be baptized to fulfill all righteousness—to be obedient. He is an example to all of us, isn't He? Ah, look there children!"

The children watched as John took Jesus by the hand and gradually lowered Him into the water, until it covered His body completely. As John slowly lifted Him out again, it seemed the very heavens opened. The clouds parted, and light was everywhere.

Gracefully and slowly, a white dove fluttered from the skies. Swooping lightly, it came to rest on the shoulder of the newly baptized Messiah, and there it remained for a time, tranquil and still.

Then, a voice of perfect peace filled the earth and sky: "This is my beloved son in whom I am well pleased." The words were like a song of love.

Katie, Matthew, and Peter knelt at the edge of the river, transfixed by what they were seeing and hearing. Nearby, Seth and his family clung to each other, equally overcome.

"It happened just the way we have always read," Katie marveled, gripping Matthew's hand.

Matthew squeezed her back and promised, "I will never forget this moment, Katie. Never." Then, using his free hand, he reached out for Peter and drew him into their embrace.

At the very instant their hands joined together, all three children suddenly felt their feet leave the ground and the air begin to swirl around them. Away from the quiet crowd, away from the river, away from the wilderness they flew. And faintly, in the distance, the sound of Grandma's voice could be heard.

Chapter Eleven

Home Again

Before there was time to wonder what was happening, Matthew, Katie, and Peter found themselves, wearing their normal clothes, sitting again on the blankets and pillows at Grandma's feet—and she was still reading!

"'And John bare record, saying, I saw the Spirit descending from heaven like a dove, and it abode upon him. And I knew him not: But he that sent me to baptize with water, the same said unto me, Upon whom thou shalt see the spirit descending, and remaining on him, the same is he which baptizeth with the Holy Ghost. And I saw, and bare record that this is the Son of God.'"

She looked up and slowly closed the Bible. The children looked at each other, bewildered. Was it possible that Grandma hadn't noticed their disappearance . . . or their sudden return?

Grandma was quiet for a moment and then looked down at her grandchildren. She began softly, "I love reading that story. It brings such peace to my heart that I feel as though I am actually there, on the banks of the River Jordan."

"I know what that feels like," said Peter.

"So do I," said Katie, while Matthew nodded.

Grandma beamed as she asked the children, "Have you thought about what you are going to write in your journals?"

"I'm going to write about the things I need to do to be baptized," Peter began. "To start with, I need to repent for the times I haven't obeyed my mom right away."

"I'm going to write about when John the Baptist was born. I didn't know his mother was so old. It must have been hard for her," said Katie.

"I think I'll write about Jesus being baptized and the dove that came from heaven," added Matthew, remembering the peace he had felt when he saw the beautiful bird alight on the Savior.

"Oh, and I'm going to tell all about the friends I made by the river!" Peter said with enthusiasm.

"Friends?" asked Grandma. "What friends?"

"Uh . . . well, I mean . . . I guess I know how the children who were there must have felt. It's almost like I know them," Peter stammered.

Grandma sighed. "I think I'll write about how I felt when I saw John baptizing Jesus in the river."

"What did you say, Grandma?" Katie quickly asked.

"Oh . . . um . . ." Now Grandma seemed flustered. "I mean . . . I'm going to write about how I felt the first time I *heard* about John baptizing Jesus." Katie kept looking right at Grandma. Was there something she wasn't telling?

"Grandma," inquired Katie, "have you ever looked at one of your paintings and thought you could see the people move?"

"Oh, not anymore, Katie," said Grandma

wistfully. "But when I was your age, it was all very real to me."

She closed her eyes and smiled, as if she were remembering. After a moment, she opened them again and stood up. "Hot chocolate sounds good, doesn't it, children? I'll go make some while you write." And with that, Grandma went out the cottage door, leaving the children alone.

Katie and the boys looked at each other. Peter was the first to ask the question. "Do you think she knows?"

"I'm not sure," said Matthew. "Think about what she wrote on the first page of our journals: 'Believe and you're there.'"

Katie chimed in, "I thought that just meant that if we really used our imaginations, it would *seem* like we were in the story. Maybe it means more than that."

"But I don't think she even knew that we were gone," Matthew was thinking out loud.

"Mom says grandmas always know more than you think," offered Peter.

Matthew added doubtfully, "I get the feeling she's not going to tell us even if we ask."

"Not today," sighed Katie, "but maybe someday."

The children picked up their pens. On the very first page of their empty journals, Katie, Matthew, and Peter began to eagerly record the feelings in their hearts. They wanted to remember this peace and love forever. Three pens busily scratched away.

"Today," began Matthew, "I stood on the banks of the River Jordan as a white dove descended from heaven."

Meanwhile, beyond the pine trees, through the garden, across the lawn and over the flagstone path, Grandma stood in the kitchen, pouring four mugs of steaming chocolate with a knowing smile on her face.

About the Authors

Alice W. Johnson, a published author and composer, is a featured speaker for youth groups, adult firesides, and women's seminars. A former executive in a worldwide strategy consulting company, and then in a leadership training firm, Alice is now a homemaker living in Eagle, Idaho, with her husband and their four young children.

Allison H. Warner gained her early experience living with her family in countries around the world. Returning to the United States as a young woman, she began her vocation as an actress and writer, developing and performing in such productions as *The Farley Family Reunion*. She and her husband reside in Provo, Utah, where they are raising two active boys.

About the Illustrator

Jerry Harston holds a degree in graphic design and has illustrated more than thirty children's books. He has received many honors for his art, and his clients include numerous Fortune 500 corporations. Jerry and his wife, Libby, live in Sandy, Utah. Their six children and sixteen grandchildren serve as excellent critics for his illustrations.